Colors

Contents

 Look and put the sticker.

red

purple

blue

orange

 Put sticker on the word.

What color is it?

It's [red] .

 Ask and say.

 Color and say.

purple

orange

blue

purple

yellow

red

orange

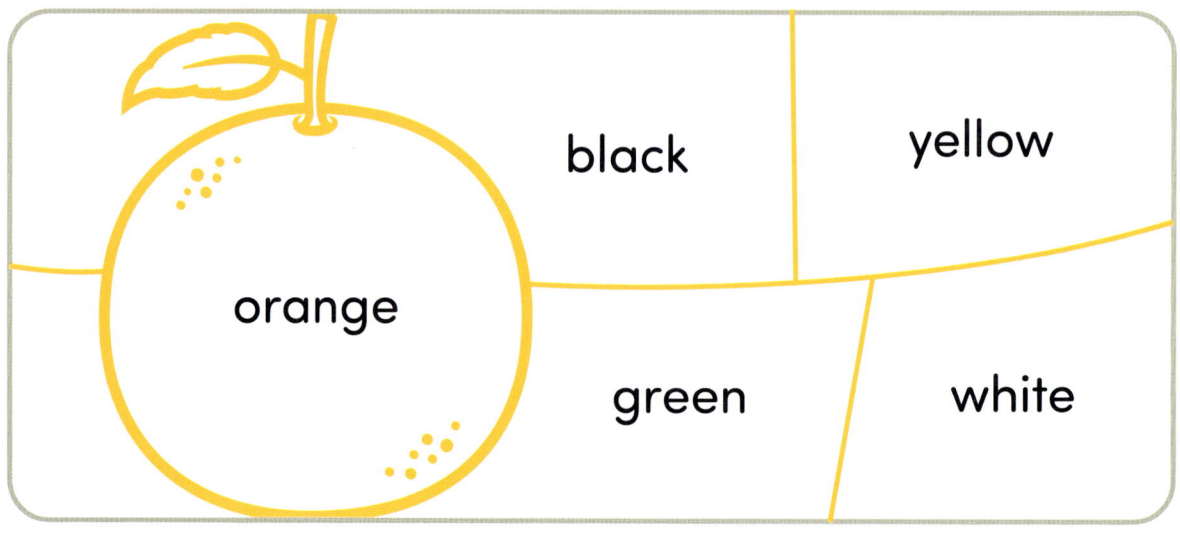

black

yellow

orange

green

white

Look and put the sticker.

black

green

yellow

white

 **Put sticker on the word.**

What color is it?

It's yellow .

 Ask and say.

red

 yellow

Color.

red

green

 Decorate the turtle.

Chatterbox Kids

orange	red
green	yellow

purple	blue
white	black